Reading Roundabout

What I Like to Wear

Paul Humphrey

Photography by Chris Fairclough

FRANKLIN WATTS
LONDON • SYDNEY

First published in 2005 by
Franklin Watts
96 Leonard Street
London EC2A 4XD

Franklin Watts Australia
Level 17/207 Kent Street
Sydney NSW 2000

ISBN 0 7496 6180 1 (hbk)
ISBN 0 7496 6192 5 (pbk)

Dewey classification number: 391

A CIP catalogue record for this book is available
from the British Library.

Planning and production by Discovery Books Limited
Editor: Rachel Tisdale
Designer: Ian Winton
Photography: Chris Fairclough
Series advisors: Diana Bentley MA and Dee Reid MA,
Fellows of Oxford Brookes University

The author, packager and publisher would like to thank the following
people for their participation in this book: Ottilie, Penny, Auriel and
Sauka Austin-Baker.

Printed in China

Contents

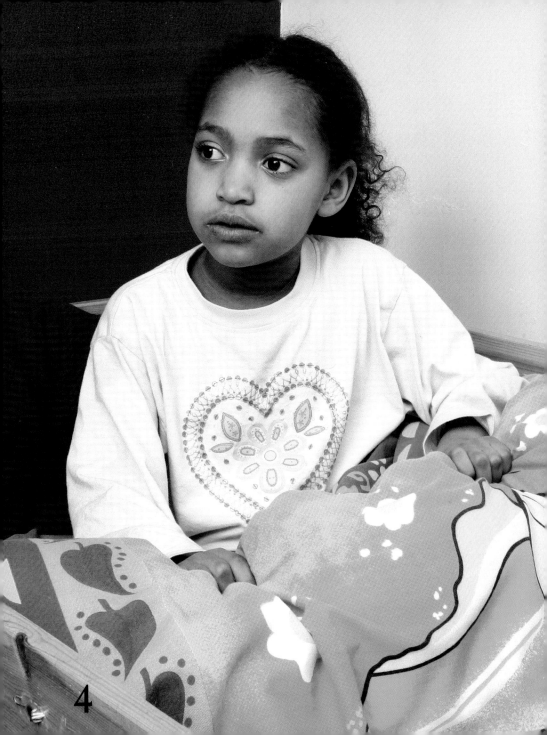

4

What shall I wear today?

When it's sunny, I like to wear my shorts and T-shirt.

7

When it's
raining, I
wear my
raincoat
and boots.

8

9

When we go
to the beach,
I wear my
swimsuit.

11

When it's cold,
I wear a warm
jumper.

I've got a cap for hot days ...

14

... and a hat for cold days.

16

When I ride
my bike, I wear
trousers and
a helmet.

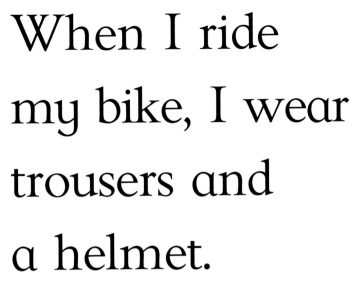

I like dressing
up in skirts and
pretty gloves
with my sisters.

When I go
to a party,
I wear
my best
shoes.

21

Today, it's snowing!
I'll need lots of clothes.

23

Word bank

Look back for these words and pictures.

Boots

Cap

Hat

Helmet

Jumper

Raincoat

Shoes

Shorts

Skirts

Swimsuit

Trousers

T-shirt

24